Hard Labor

The First African Americans, 1619

BY PATRICIA C. McKISSACK & FREDRICK L. McKISSACK JR.

ILLUSTRATED BY JOSEPH DANIEL FIEDLER

ALADDIN

New York   London   Toronto   Sydney   Singapore

John, James Everett, and Peter
Sarah, Jasmine, and MaJon

First Aladdin Library edition January 2004
Text copyright © 2004 by Patricia C. McKissack & Fredrick L. McKissack Jr.
Illustrations copyright © 2004 by Joseph Daniel Fiedler

ALADDIN PAPERBACKS
An imprint of Simon & Schuster Children's Publishing Division
1230 Avenue of the Americas, New York, NY 10020

Also available in an Aladdin Paperbacks edition.
Designed by Debra Sfetsios
The text of this book was set in Cheltenham.

Printed in the United States of America
2 4 6 8 10 9 7 5 3 1

Library of Congress Control Number 2003110501

ISBN 0-689-86150-8

PREFACE

WHEN WE started researching for this book, we had ideas and opinions about how we should approach the subject. Our goal was to tell the story of the first generation of African people who came to the New World. It's not possible to tell the story without discussing slavery, and that's a very difficult subject to write about. Reading about it too can be equally as stressful. Visions of chains and whips, harsh words and cruel deeds can cause feelings of anger, fear, hurt, or embarrassment. That is not what we wanted to do.

This book celebrates the lives of those Africans who are the founding fathers and mothers of the African-American population. Many of them, we learned, arrived in chains, but some made the journey as freemen. Black hands helped explore, settle, and develop this great country, yet information about them—even their names—has been erased by time. Stories about them are often incomplete and the facts blurred by centuries of neglect. But these stories are worth knowing and keeping and sharing. Their trials and triumphs are a part of the whole American saga. That's what this book is about.

Africans in America endured many hardships in a faraway and often hostile land. Nevertheless, they managed to resist all attempts to destroy their will to survive. Their survival is a testimony to the resilience of the human spirit. That, too, is what this book is about.

PATRICIA C. MCKISSACK

FREDRICK L. MCKISSACK JR.

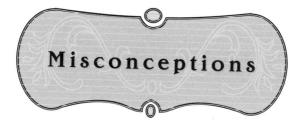

Misconceptions

WHEN DID the first Africans arrive in the New World? Where did they come from? How did they come? What happened to them?

Historians, archaeologists, theologians, writers, and many others continue to search for answers to these difficult questions. Though we have learned a great deal because of their research, the records are still incomplete and scholars disagree about details. Misunderstandings continue.

A common error is the belief that slavery began in the New World and that Africans were the first to be enslaved. However, the buying and selling of human beings dates back to ancient times. It was practiced in Africa, Asia, Europe, the Middle East, and among the Indians of North and South America long before Columbus's voyage in 1492.

Another misconception is that 1619 is the date that slaves arrived in North America. Twenty Africans were brought to Jamestown, Virginia, in that year and sold to the colonists. True. Jamestown in 1619 is a milestone year, because it is the beginning of African-American history in the British colonies.

But that's not the whole story.

The Jamestown Africans were sold as indentured servants, not slaves. Indentured servitude had been going on in Europe and Britain for centuries. After serving for seven years, an indentured servant was freed.

When Britain entered the slave market, some Africans were forced to become indentured servants, like the ones brought to Jamestown. Some of these early Africans in America became Virginia landowners and craftsmen after they served their time. A few even had indentured servants of their own.

However, the Jamestown Africans weren't the first blacks to set foot in the New World. There is convincing evidence there was an African presence in South America before Columbus. While that is being researched and debated, we know for sure that men of African descent—some free, some servants, and some slaves—accompanied Spanish and Portuguese conquistadors and clergy in voyages of exploration. They witnessed the awesome beauty of the land—snowcapped mountain ranges, valleys, plains, and seashores filled with all kinds of unusual

wildlife and plants. They were there and saw it all.

Later, as Europeans began settling the New World, a new generation of Africans made the Atlantic crossing. This time they were captives chained in the bellies of ships. Planters needed a cheap labor force to make their sugarcane, tobacco, and rice plantations profitable. Slavery provided an answer. Trying to enslave the Indians didn't work. But in Africa there seemed to be an endless supply of laborers.

Plenty of European, Arab, and African investors saw an opportunity to get rich fast in the slave trade. As the demand for new workers increased, profits soared. So did the kidnappings. So did the midnight raids on African villages. So did the terror of the slave ships. In the end, millions of Africans were dispersed throughout the New World lands. African peoples left an indelible mark on the pages of American history. And their contributions cannot be denied.

To understand the importance of 1619 as a milestone year in America, you must begin in Europe and Africa during the fifteenth and sixteenth centuries. Think of this as a board game. The first move is to get a clear definition of "slave" and "slavery." Then keep advancing until you reach the destination of Jamestown, Virginia, 1619—a very important date to remember. Ready for the first move?

CHAPTER ONE

Slavery without Race

WHAT IS a slave? When and where did slavery start? How was it practiced?

Quite simply, slaves are men, women, and children who are owned by other people. Slaves have no rights and they aren't paid for their work.

In ancient times if a white man and a black man were walking down the street together, there was no way to determine who was the slave and who was the master. Race was not a condition of slavery.

Back then *anybody* could be captured and sold—even a king. The color of a person's skin had very little to do with his or her being enslaved. That idea would be developed much later.

A person was enslaved for different reasons. The usual one was conquest. When one nation defeated another, often the foreign captives were sold for profit. Sometimes criminals were made to work for no pay for a period of time as their punishment. So were those who owed money they couldn't repay or whose religious beliefs were prohibited by those in power. Very often, being put on the slave block silenced a person who opposed the ruling class.

In some cultures, an unmarried young man might voluntarily become the unpaid servant of a rich man who agreed in exchange to take care of the boy's widowed mother and sisters. There was usually a limit of four to seven years placed on the time of this kind of servitude. This was called indentured service.

Daughters were sometimes bartered as slave wives to pay off the debts or taxes of their families. In some instances a young man might bind himself to a craftsman in exchange for learning a trade.

One of the earliest civilizations to use slaves on a vast scale was Egypt. Unpaid workers built the Pyramids and other great structures like temples and monuments. In 221 B.C. the emperor Qin Shi Huangdi used "forced labor" to build the Great Wall of China.

In Europe the ancient Greeks had a large slave population. Then the Romans defeated the Greeks and enslaved them as well as other people throughout the known world. In fact, the term slave comes from the "slavs" of middle Europe who were enslaved by Romans.

In northern Europe a serf was a slave with a more acceptable name. People were bound to the land owned by a nobleman in exchange for protection. At the same time that Europeans were stumbling through the Dark Ages, thousands of miles away in Mexico and Central and South America, captives of the Aztec, Mayan, and Inca empires were constructing great cities and monuments that are still standing today. Southern Spain was experiencing a golden age under the rule of conquering Moorish (black) kings of North Africa. And farther south there was a vigorous slave trade between the Middle East and the African kingdoms below the Sahara Desert. Slave hands mined gold and salt, which were the sources of great wealth in medieval Ghana and Mali.

Among the numerous African groups,

there were rules that governed the treatment of slaves by their masters. Slave owners were ordered by law to feed, clothe, and provide their slaves with shelter. Slaves were to be trained. They were allowed to marry, sometimes into the master's family. They could be adopted and inherit property and titles. Above all, their children were born free. No unborn child was doomed to be owned because his or her parents were. In some African societies slaves could be freed, then advance within that society to become generals, business owners, even kings.

When Europeans reached West African shores below the Sahara in the fifteenth century, slavery was well established and accepted all over the world in one form or another.

CHAPTER TWO

The Age of Exploration Begins

WHEN DID Europeans make contact with Africans? When were Africans taken away from their homeland as slaves?

Before the 1440s, an unfriendly ocean and a sea of sand protected West Africa. The ocean currents would not allow ships to sail down the coast of Africa and then back again. The only way to reach African empires below the Sahara was by a long and dangerous journey through the scorching desert patrolled by scorpions and bandits.

A few books were written by Arab travelers that raised the interest of Europeans. Al-Bakri and Ibn Battuta's accounts described a gold-rich land, abundant in exotic plants, unusual animals, and interesting people. For centuries the rumors of such a place persisted. Except for a few curiosity seekers and those few blacks that had been sold to Europeans through Arab slave traders, European contact with Africa was limited.

Prince Henry of Portugal had a love of adventure, an interest in sailing vessels, and a longing for power and fame. At his school of navigation he inspired Portuguese captains who shared his vision to seek out new and better trade routes. Here, they also invented a sail that made a voyage down the coast of Africa possible. These voyages ushered in the age of exploration. The new sails were tested when Ruy de Pina reached Benin in 1486, and Diego Cao explored the inner regions of the Congo in 1482. Captains

sailed around Africa from west to east and back again, returning to Lisbon with cargoes of ivory, cloth, and *slaves.*

By all accounts the stories about Africa were true. The Africans were knowledgeable about farming, fishing, weaving, medicine, sculpture, marketing, blacksmithing, architecture, religion, and much more. They spoke different languages and practiced different religions, including Islam. Some knew about Christianity and Judaism. The Portuguese were amazed that in a few African cities there were great mosques, universities, and libraries. African peoples below the Sahara also had sophisticated trade systems with their Berber and Arab neighbors.

Other ships followed, and soon the Portuguese had a trade system that included a modest slave trade.

Slavery at that time was a class system.

Remember, slaves were not slaves simply because they were Africans. While captives from Benin, Congo, Angola, and Mali were being sold, other Africans were being entertained by royalty in European capitals. Africa, Europe, and the Middle East exchanged students, languages, goods, and ideas. But that didn't last very long.

Portugal and Spain took the lead during the age of exploration. Little did anybody know how much it would impact Africa and her people.

CHAPTER THREE

They Came with the Conquistadors

WHO WERE the first blacks to come to the Americas? When did they come? Why did they come?

People of African descent came to the Americas with the conquistadors—some free, some servants, and some slaves. They were Afro-Spanish, Afro-Portuguese, and from many different African cultures.

The Moors (blacks) of Morocco in North Africa had conquered and ruled southern Spain for nearly five hundred years. Then Queen Isabella and King Ferdinand, the rulers of Castile and Aragon, defeated the

Moorish king at Granada in 1492—a pivotal year. Spain was unified as a Christian nation. Driven by her religious zeal, Queen Isabella issued the Edict of Expulsion that same year. The edict specifically singled out Jews, but eventually all non-Christians were ordered to convert to Christianity or leave Spain. In order to save their homes and businesses, some Jews and Muslims publicly converted, but practiced their own religion secretly. They were dealt with harshly when discovered.

Thousands of other Muslim Spaniards returned to their North African homeland. They poured into overcrowded cities such as Fez, putting a strain on the economy and resources there. People died from despair and disease. Before long the welcome mat was pulled out from under them. Where could they go? Many turned toward the sea.

Muslims, Christians, and Jews eagerly

joined the crews of exploration ships. Not for adventure. Not for riches. Not for fame. They signed up to escape religious persecution.

Africans and Islamic Afro-Spaniards were a part of Christopher Columbus's crew, who were looking for a shorter trade route to India and to spread the glory of God. And, of course, if any gold was found along the way, that would be fine.

After months of traveling west on the stormy seas of the Atlantic Ocean, Columbus's three weary ships reached an island. There were water, food, and Indians. The year was 1492. We all know the story well. Little is known about the crewmembers of the *Niña,* the *Pinta,* and the *Santa María.* But the pilot of Columbus's flagship, *Santa María*, was Pedro Alonzo Nino, a man of African descent.

Columbus returned to Spain and immediately began preparing for another voyage.

Other adventurers outfitted ships and sailed out with multiracial crews. Men of all races, colors, and religions joined them—some free, some servants, some slaves.

Records show that Nuflo de Olano and twenty-nine other black men were with the great Spanish explorer Balboa when he reached the Pacific Ocean. Olano was a servant, but his presence must have been significant, because he was named. Rarely were slaves or servants mentioned in official records except to record their numbers.

In 1513 blacks accompanied another Spanish explorer, Juan Ponce de León, in his search for the Fountain of Youth. They were probably the ones who helped plant the orange and lemon trees in what would later become Florida. Black men came with Francisco Pizarro, a conquistador who sailed from Panama to explore Peru in 1531. They were with Hernán Cortés when he completed the Spanish conquest of Mexico—New Spain—in 1527. And they were part of García López de Cárdenas's party in 1540 when they looked in awe at the Grand Canyon.

These servants of the conquistadors carried the supplies and hacked paths through thick and tangled brush. They took care of the animals and did most of the cooking. And when necessary, they took up arms and defended the group.

These faceless men experienced the same hardships as their leaders and marveled at the same wonderful things they saw. Both slave and master struggled with the fear of the unknown. Each endured the heat and humidity, fought mosquitoes and gnats, suffered the pangs of hunger, got sick from diseases, and died in Indian attacks. Yet slaves' names are not mentioned in

history books. Olano was an exception.

Another notable African explorer was Estévanico (Esteban the Moor). His story reads like an adventure novel beginning in Morocco where he was purchased as a slave by a Spanish explorer. He landed in Florida and survived a hurricane, but he was captured by Indians in Texas and enslaved. He learned their language and escaped to freedom. He traveled the Southwest in search of the Seven Cities of Gold. Among the Pima Indians there, he was thought to be a god until he tried to escape. He was killed.

Not much more is known about the first blacks that came to the Americas. Still, time has not been able to erase their existence. They are remembered whenever Native Americans tell their stories about the coming of the conquistadors—especially the ones who had black skin.

CHAPTER FOUR

Sugar and Slaves

WHEN WERE Africans brought to the Americas as slaves? Where? Why?

The Spanish and Portuguese conquistadors conquered the land in the name of their monarchs. Next came settlers who established colonies, and priests who started missions. Columbus's brother established the colony of Santo Domingo on the island of Hispaniola in 1498. Other colonies followed. When the mining of gold and other minerals failed, the colonial powers needed to find a commodity that had great commercial value to make colonization worth the investment.

They soon found a gold mine in sugar.

Sugarcane was harvested on Hispaniola in 1506. When sugar was produced a few years later in Havana, planters quickly realized there were three things needed to guarantee high profits: demand for the product, climate, and labor force. The first two factors were in place.

Europeans had a "sweet tooth," and the demand for sugar was high. The Caribbean Islands and Brazil had excellent growing conditions. The soil was rich, the growing season was long, and the climate was hot and humid. Perfect for growing sugarcane.

The success of the crop largely depended on a big labor force. To guarantee higher profits, Spanish authorities decided to use slave labor.

At first, planters tried enslaving Indians. But that plan didn't work. The Indians were rapidly dying out from smallpox, measles, and even the common cold. Others resisted. They ran away or led rebellions.

In 1510 a shipload of blacks was brought from Africa to work in Brazil. In 1512 Africans were taken to Hispaniola. Word spread that Africans seemed to adapt better to the hot and steamy conditions in the fields, which were not unlike their own African climates.

In an effort to save the lives of the few remaining Arawak Indians on Hispaniola, Bishop Bartolomé de Las Casas, a missionary, suggested in 1517 that enslaving Africans would be better than enslaving the Indians, who were near extinction. His arguments were so convincing that in 1518 a license was given to Lorens de Gominot by the Spanish crown. He was allowed to take four thousand African slaves to the Caribbean. They weren't

enslaved because they'd committed crimes. Not because of unpaid debts. Not because of religious differences. Not even because they were black. Africans were selected to be slaves at that time because they were available. Las Casas later regretted having supported and argued this idea.

The irony is that in May of that same year Henry of the Congo led a mission to the Vatican. He formally addressed the pope in Latin and was appointed bishop of the Congo. But the lure of wealth silenced any opposition to slavery. Even when Pope Leo X passed a declaration in 1514 against slavery, it did nothing to stop the steady flow of slave ships. Soon even priests were involved in the sale of human beings.

The holocaust known as the transatlantic slave trade had begun. What started as a trickle, soon became a tidal wave.

CHAPTER FIVE

Permanent Settlements

WHERE WERE the first permanent settlements in North America? Were blacks a part of these settlements?

This second wave of Africans who came to the Americas was very different from those who came with the conquistadors. Those who came in slave ships and were sold to planters in the Caribbean and Brazil had a life expectancy of two years. They were forced to work endless hours in the sugarcane fields.

As plantations popped up like mushrooms, speculators looked for additional land to cultivate. Why not North America? In the summer of 1526 Lucas Vásquez de Ayllón and five hundred fellow Spaniards and one hundred black slaves left Hispaniola in hopes of expanding Spain's sugar empire north. They founded San Miguel de Guadalupe near the mouth of the Pee Dee River at Winyah Bay, South Carolina.

Most of the group died of diseases or fell during Indian attacks. The Cherokee were familiar with the Spanish conquistadors who had tried to make slaves of them. They also knew about blacks, because Hernando de Soto's soldiers had captured the Lady of Cofitachiqui, a great Cherokee leader. She escaped with the help of a Spanish officer's African slave. The black man was welcomed into the tribe as her husband.

Disease and attack further weakened the colonists. The slaves seized the opportunity and rebelled against their masters. Escaping into the wilderness they joined forces with the Indians.

Recognizing defeat, the few surviving Spaniards abandoned the settlement in less than six months and retreated to Hispaniola. The blacks they left behind married Indians. Their racially mixed great-grandchildren would be among those who witnessed the arrival of the English settlers a century later.

Meanwhile, other nations were now joining the competition for the American land grab. For decades the Spanish and Portuguese had dominated the New World. But not anymore. In 1564 a group of French Huguenots built Fort Caroline on the St. Johns River on the western shore of Florida. Like the Muslims and Jews of Spain, these French Protestants left their homeland to escape religious persecution. When the Spanish

king heard about the settlement, he sent Pedro Menéndez de Avilés to destroy the French fort. After destroying it, Avilés set up St. Augustine, which is said to be the first permanent European settlement in the United States. Once again, blacks were part of that settlement, serving in the capacity of servant and slave.

There may have been a few blacks that were part of the first and second settlements at Roanoke Island, Virginia. The first colony established in 1584–85 by Sir Walter Raleigh was abandoned. A second colony was established in 1587. When a supply ship returned on August 17, 1590, all the settlers had vanished with only the clues "CRO" and "CROATOAN" carved in nearby trees. Blacks were definitely a part of the Jamestown colony.

CHAPTER SIX

Jamestown, 1607

WHEN WAS Jamestown settled?

England was slow in joining the age of exploration and the slave trade. A few individuals, such as John Hawkins, were heavily involved in the African-Caribbean slave market as early as 1562. Queen Elizabeth gave her approval to Hawkins, who shared his profits with the Queen. Although he was a swashbuckling scoundrel and a privateer, the queen was grateful. She knighted him and his coat of arms was an African in chains.

Queen Elizabeth used the profits from slave sales to pay for her war against the

Spanish. In 1588 England defeated the great Spanish navy, the Armada. Thereafter England ruled the seas. Queen Elizabeth turned her attention to the Americas and expansion of the British Empire. It was work that would be completed by her successors.

It wasn't difficult to convince business-men to invest in colonization ventures. And the idea of going to a place where dreams might be fulfilled was very appealing. It was a great concept that worked. The Virginia Company of London, an investment group, sponsored the Jamestown expedition.

In April 1607, Captain John Smith led 120 English colonists, including their indentured servants, to the shores of Virginia. They founded Jamestown, the first permanent *English* settlement in North America. The name honored the ruling monarch, King James. Other ships came and brought more men,

women, and children. Though 900 people had arrived, 1610 saw only 60 people left alive.

It wasn't as easy as they had thought it would be. They suffered many hardships, including Indian attacks, starvation, and diseases. This was called the "starving time." Captain John Smith's courage and determination helped them survive.

Then in 1612 John Rolfe successfully planted, harvested, and cured tobacco. In 1617 the first shipment of tobacco was sent to London. A few years later nearly 55,000 pounds of it was exported to England. At last the investment was paying off. Although King James said tobacco was nothing more than an unhealthy, "noxious weed" that "watered the eyes" and "caused a cough," the English were hooked on it.

Tobacco plantations flourished. The Virginia colony was so successful, investors wanted to sponsor other settlements. But in order to be competitive, Virginia planters needed a work force equal to that of the sugar planters in the Caribbean. Should they use slaves?

They decided to use indentured servants instead. At first they were mostly fellow Englishmen who were brought to Virginia, where they were bound to work for another person for four to seven years to pay off their passage or some other debt or obligation.

Virginia planters advertised for people to come to Virginia as indentured servants. They were promised food, clothing, and shelter. If they lived to complete their service, they would receive a bushel of corn, a new suit, and a small piece of land.

People who were starving on the streets of London thought this sounded like a good deal. Criminals were given the choice of either going to the Americas as an indentured servant or going to the dreaded prisons of Europe. All kinds of men and women were indentured. For some it was a chance to start over. How bad could it be?

Very bad!

In August of 1619—a full year before the Pilgrims reached Massachusetts on the *Mayflower*—John Rolfe wrote in his journal that there "came in a Dutch man of warre that sold us twenty Negars." The captain offered to trade the Africans for food and water.

The twenty Africans were probably captured in the Congo and loaded on a Spanish slave ship bound for the Caribbean. But this Dutch vessel had robbed them of their cargo and ended up in Jamestown with them.

The Africans who were sold as indentured servants began a new page in the history of Africans in America.

CHAPTER SEVEN

Indentured Servitude

HOW WERE indentured servants treated?

The Jamestown Africans had been baptized and given Spanish names before arriving in Virginia. Though they had been robbed of their freedom, they had not been denied basic human rights, such as the right to get married and parent children. Documents show that among the first Africans there was an "Antonio" and an "Isabella." These two people married and in 1623 the couple's son, William, was born. William was christened in the Church of England. He holds the distinction of being the first child of African descent born in British North American colonies. What is important to remember is, William was born free.

Antonio and Isabella weren't treated differently from any of the white indentured servants. Their skin color didn't help or hinder their situation. Life for white and black indentured servants was equally harsh.

There were no laws about how servants were to be treated or the responsibilities of a master. Treatment was based on the personality of each master. Kind people treated their servants kindly. Unkind people tended to be cruel, even brutal.

As harsh as life was, indentured servants still had hope, because at that time slavery was not a life sentence. There was a limit on how long they could be held—four, seven, ten, twenty years. Antonio and Isabella knew that if they could hold on, eventually they would be free. Once free, they could own land, vote, testify in court, and hold public office.

This system was familiar to Africans and so they seemingly eased into the rhythm of the socioeconomic structure of Jamestown.

After the Dutch ship delivered those first indentured servants to Jamestown, other ships named the *James* and the *Margrett and John* followed. They brought other Europeans and more Africans. They joined those who were already working in the tobacco fields of Virginia. Their names appear in old records, log books, court documents. In 1625 Brase, "a Negro," arrived. John Pedro, an Afro-Spaniard, arrived on the *Swan* in 1623. In 1624, a black man, John Phillip, testified in a Jamestown court. He was allowed to do so, because "he had been christened in England twelve years since."

Meanwhile other colonies were being settled along the eastern seashore of North America, places such as Plymouth, Massachusetts, and New Netherlands (later to become New York). Africans took part in the growth of these colonies as well.

One of the first legal cases in the colonies involves eleven black men who were indentured to the Dutch West Indian Company. They petitioned to be provided wives. The company agreed and imported three women, identified as "Angolans." Other women followed and African-American families began to emerge.

In New York, now controlled by the British, black indentured servants filed a petition for freedom in 1644, claiming they had been held beyond the terms of their indenture. They won their case and were freed. All received parcels of land in what is now Greenwich Village.

These and other incidents show that while Africans in the Caribbean and South America were suffering horrific treatment at the hands of their masters, Africans in North America were being integrated into the mainstream of society. They lived among the English, worked side by side, sharing knowledge and helping each other in the struggle against the elements.

One of the most significant contributions the first Africans made was to help eliminate the threat of starvation. In an official document, the governor of Virginia ordered rice to be planted in 1648 "on the advice of our Negroes." He was told that the conditions for growing rice in Virginia were the same as in "their country." Rice became a profitable export, and a staple commodity in the colonial diet, thanks to African captives.

CHAPTER EIGHT

Anthony Johnson

IN 1622, as part of a major Indian uprising, Powhatan Indians attacked the Bennett Plantation along the James River. When it was over, fifty-five colonists were dead. One of five survivors was an indentured servant called Antonio. Is this the same Antonio who was married to Isabella, the father of William? Some historians believe that it is. Others disagree.

It is hard to be sure, because there were so many Anthonys, Antonios, Antoneys, and Tonys listed in official papers. Spellings changed, even within the same document,

and last names were not always used to identify families.

At some point, however, an "Antonio" became Anthony Johnson. After years of research, historians have painstakingly pieced together the life of one Anthony (Antonio) Johnson.

Anthony was also an indentured servant. He probably came from Angola in Africa to England to Virginia, arriving in Jamestown on the *James* in 1621. That same year, "Mary, a Negro woman" arrived onboard the *Margrett and John*. Records show Anthony and Mary married in 1623.

No more is heard about the Johnsons until 1641. By that time they had served out their indenture and had become landowners. In fact, Anthony was an owner of servants himself. One was John Casor.

As he prospered, he acquired more

servants. By 1651 he held the indenture contracts on five servants, several of whom were white.

He was granted 250 acres of land on the south side of the Pungoteague Creek in Northampton County, according to the "headrights" system: Planters were given deed to 50 acres of land for each person, or "head," brought to the colony as a worker.

In 1652 John Johnson, Anthony's son, imported or acquired through purchase eleven persons and received 550 acres. Another son acquired two white indentured servants and received 100 acres.

The Johnson compound became the first African-American community. Johnson was a well-respected resident and praised in a court document for his "hard work and known service."

The Johnson family story is extraordinary.

Most people could not boast his accomplishments. Clearly it illustrates that in the early years of North American colonization, it was possible for an indentured servant to become successful regardless of race. Unfortunately, that was about to change.

Chapter Nine

Racism and Slavery

WHEN DID racism become a part of slavery?

Colonial officials were concerned with two things: profits and peace. Profits were the driving force behind most of their decisions. And keeping the peace ensured that all operations ran smoothly and efficiently so that profits would continue to be made. Caribbean planters were outproducing British farms in the colonies by a wide margin because they used chattel slavery—slaves for life.

To stay competitive, the British colonial government petitioned and received the right to enter the African slave trade more aggressively.

It was purely an economic decision. Racism, for the time being, remained a personal matter and the government didn't sanction the idea.

Racism is a form of prejudice. It has existed since humankind first encountered "differences." No doubt there were colonists who, without reason, resented or feared Africans and Indians because they belonged to a different race. And vice versa. This kind of racial prejudice wasn't reflected in the colonial common law. (These were rules and laws that dictated the way people were governed on a day-to-day basis.)

Attitudes about Africans began to change gradually. Slave dealers created an image of Africa as a wild and uncivilized place where heathens and savages lived.

Religious leaders who suggested God cursed black people assisted in the dehumanization of Africans. That they were created to be "a servant race" or that they "deserved" to be slaves for some sin committed in a Bible story by one of Noah's sons became popular notions.

If a lie is spoken often enough, it will begin to sound like the truth. Soon these racist notions found their way into the mainstream. People began accepting as truth that they were doing Africans a favor by enslaving them.

As racist attitudes became more acceptable, laws were changed to reflect those beliefs.

In 1641 Massachusetts became the first colony to legalize chattel slavery. Connecticut followed in 1650 and Virginia in 1661. Shortly thereafter Virginia passed a law

stating that a child born to a slave mother would also be a slave.

For the first time Europeans no longer defined themselves as just "Christians." For the first time Europeans used skin color to define and separate themselves. Being "white" meant being "superior" to all others. Without reason or proof, dark-skinned people—Africans and Indians—were different and, based on this criteria, assigned to an "inferior" race.

Two incidents help to illustrate how shifting attitudes shaped new laws. In 1640 three indentured servants belonging to Hugh Gwyn, a farmer, escaped. They were captured and brought back to Jamestown. All three were equal in status. All three were beaten. Then Victor, a Dutchman, and James Gregory, a Scotsman, were each sentenced to serve out their indentures plus one year more, and to serve the colony for three additional years after that. The judge passed sentence on the third man, a black man, saying, "...being a [N]egro named John Punch shall serve his said master or his assigns for the time of his natural life."

For the time of his natural life.

There is no case on record where a white servant was sentenced to be a slave for life. Punch was the first recorded in Virginia. Why? He had done no more wrong than his fellow runaways had. The difference was that Punch was the "wrong" color. The fact that the sentence was not challenged or appealed indicates that such bias was acceptable. It was a prelude to racism.

The second incident to further undermine the rights of African citizenry was a slave uprising. On September 13, 1663, white and black indentured servants planned a revolt.

They were betrayed by one of their own.

Disturbed by the possibility of future uprisings, slaveholders began demanding laws that allowed them to manage their slaves more strictly. The colonial government responded.

In 1663 a Virginia court ruled that when a child was born to a slave mother, the child was a slave automatically. Blacks could no longer own white slaves, and interracial marriages were forbidden. Fearful that their fates would be interlocked with blacks, poor whites began distancing themselves. In their thinking, it was better to be poor than black. Now, where there once had been natural alliances and partnerships, suspicion and mistrust emerged.

Of course, the division between the white indentured servants and slaves was to the advantage of the masters. By keeping the two races separate and in conflict with each other, the ruling class kept the peace and raked in the profits.

CHAPTER TEN

The End of an Era

WHAT HAPPENED to the Johnsons?

The continued passage of restrictive slave laws must have been distressing for Anthony Johnson and his sons. He and his sons were free, but a black man had no way to "prove he was slave or free." This made traveling far from home to do business difficult for all free blacks.

Anthony had worked hard, provided for his family, and served his community well. It was time for him to reap the rewards of his labors. But in 1653 the Johnsons' farm burned. When the couple requested relief, the court agreed to exempt Mary and two daughters from county taxation. They gave as the reason Anthony's "hard work and known service." This is a testimony to the respect that Anthony Johnson commanded at that time.

Yet, even a towering presence like Anthony Johnson was not immune to radically shifting racial attitudes.

The following year a white planter, Robert Parker, helped Anthony's black slave, John Casor, get released. Casor had convinced Parker that Anthony was holding him beyond his legal indenture. Anthony fought the case and the courts returned Casor to the Johnsons in 1655.

On the heels of this decision, another planter, named Matthew Pippen, claimed that one hundred acres of Johnson's land belonged to him. Perhaps Anthony had

depleted his funds or maybe he didn't think it was worth the fight. For whatever reason, Anthony chose not to challenge Pippin's claim. Shortly after that, however, Mary and Anthony moved to Somerset County in Maryland. They rented land and called it Tonies Vineyard. Trouble followed him there.

Before leaving for South Carolina, Anthony sold some of his Virginia land to two white farmers on credit. Two years later, they paid Johnson with a portion of their tobacco crop. But a corrupt official named Edmund Scarburgh claimed that the tobacco belonged to him for payment of a loan. Anthony denied owing the debt.

Scarburgh produced a promissory note, supposedly written and signed by Johnson. Ignoring the fact that Anthony could neither read or write, the court ruled in favor of Scarburgh. He was allowed to keep the tobacco. Anthony was out of both land and payment.

It might be argued that this kind of corruption was commonplace. Whites as well as blacks were often the victims of unprincipled judges and officials. But in the case of Anthony Johnson and other African Americans during this time, racism was clearly influencing their decisions.

Anthony died in August 1670. It was a sad tribute to his hard work when an all-white jury ruled that his original Virginia land could be seized by the state "because he was a Negro and by consequence an alien."

Mary Johnson lived on Tonies Vineyard until she died a decade later. Clinging to the dying hopes of a diminishing free population of blacks, John Johnson Jr. purchased a forty-acre tract in Virginia in 1677. He named it "Angola" after his grandfather's birthplace. John Johnson Jr. died in the early 1700s, leaving no heir.

Most records of the Anthony Johnson family vanished. And the story of the first generation of African Americans who came to Jamestown remained untold and unappreciated for hundreds of years. An era of free blacks contributing to the rise of colonial America came to a sad end just as our nation was coming to the threshold of its beginning.

CONCLUSION

AFRICAN MEN and women like Anthony and Mary Johnson were no different from the thousands of other immigrants who came to this country as indentured servants. With their freedom in the foreseeable future, they dared to be hopeful. The Johnsons give us a glimmer of what might have been, had their descendants been given opportunity and fair treatment. If racism had not been attached to slavery, and if the indentured system had been used instead of chattel slavery, perhaps African people and their ancestors might have continued being good neighbors and contributing citizens. Instead the nation would take a different route. The opportunities and acceptance the Johnsons experienced would fade away and be forgotten for a time.

The next generation of Africans who came to the thirteen colonies arrived with no hope of ever being free—or their children or their children's children being free. The sentence that John Punch received was passed on the heads of millions of Africans who were destined to be "property" for the rest of "their natural lives."

The transition from indentured service to chattel slavery was complete by 1700. If a white man and black man were walking down the street together, there was no doubt about who was the slave and who was the master. The slave was assumed to be the one with the dark skin—the African. And more often than not the African *was* a slave.

Between the lines of written history are the hopes and dreams of those first "twenty odd Negroes" who landed at Jamestown. They were Africans. They became Americans. They worked hard and served the community well. Their African-American descendants are the bounty of the seeds they planted in the rich earth of a new land.

1619: A Dutch ship sells twenty slaves to the settlers at Jamestown, Virginia, in exchange for food and fresh water.

1620: Plymouth Colony in Massachusetts is founded.

1622: Powhatan attacks Jamestown Colony. Over fifty-five colonists are killed. Anthony Johnson survives the attack.

"Mary, a Negro woman," arrives in Jamestown onboard the Margrett and John. Anthony Johnson and Mary are married.

1623: William, the son of indentured sevants named Antonio and Isabella, is born free in the Jamestown Colony. (It is not known if

Antonio and Isabella are the same as Anthony and Isabella Johnson.)

1640: John Punch, an indentured servant, is sentenced by a Virginia judge to serve for all "his natural life."

1641: Anthony Johnson becomes a landowner in Jamestown. He owns an indentured servant named John Casor.

Massachusetts becomes the first colony to legalize chattel slavery (slavery for life).

1644: Black indentured servants file a petition for freedom, claiming that they have been held beyond their terms of indenture. They win their case.

1648: With the help of Africans, rice becomes a staple commodity and a profitable export.

1650: Connecticut legalizes chattel slavery.

1651: Anthony Johnson holds the indenture

contract on five servants, both black and white. He is granted 250 acres according to the "head rights system."

1652: Johnson's son John Johnson imports eleven people as indentured servants and receives 550 acres. Another son acquires two white servants and is awarded a hundred acres.

1653: Anthony Johnson's farm burns, and the court allows the family a tax break.

1654: John Casor sues Johnson claiming that Johnson has held him longer than his agreed upon indenture. The court rules in Johnson's favor.

1656–57: The Johnsons move to South Carolina.

1661–62: Virginia legalizes chattel slavery.

1662: Virginia passes a law that a child born to a slave mother will also be a slave. Such practice was not common in the civilized world.

1663: On September 13, white and black indentured servants plan a revolt. They are
betrayed by one of their own.

1670: Anthony Johnson dies.

1677: John Johnson Jr., the grandson of Mary and
Anthony Johnson, purchases forty acres
and names it "Angola."

1698: Royal African Company loses its monopoly
on the slave trade. Now slaving is open to
independent traders.

Fourth statehouse burns in Virginia.

1699: Capital of Virginia moves from Jamestown to
Williamsburg.

1700: John Johnson Jr. dies in the early 1700s and
leaves no heirs.

Chattel slavery is practiced throughout the
New World.

VIRTUAL VISITS

Explorers

    www.enchantedlearning.com

Jamestown

    www.virtualschool.edu

Blacks in Virginia

    www.nps.gov/colo/Jthanout/AFRI

Anthony Johnson

    http://mdroots.thinkport.org/library/